# THIS BOOK is for the aspirational gardener!

WHETHER YOU ARE A SERIAL PLANT MURDERER WANTING TO ADD (AND KEEP!) SOME LIFE TO YOUR ABODE OR A MORE SEASONED FOLIAGE ENTHUSIAST LOOKING FOR TIPS AND TRICKS, THE IDEA OF CULTIVATING AN INDOOR GARDEN CAN SEEM DREAMY, BUT DAUNTING. THIS HANDY GUIDE IS HERE TO HELP YOU FALL IN LOVE WITH PLANTS AND LEARN TO DOTE ON A FOREST OF YOUR VERY OWN.

# Contents

# Why we should keep plants

PLANTS ARE A WONDERFUL ADDITION
TO ANY LIVING SPACE, AND I AM A
HUGE ADVOCATE OF CULTIVATING
A PLANT PARADISE IN YOUR HOME.

IF YOU'RE NOT AS EASILY SWAYED
AS ME, HERE ARE SOME REASONS
TO GIVE IN TO THE GREENERY!

**1** PLANTS NEED LIGHT: HUMANS NEED LIGHT. THE PRESENCE OF PLANTS IN YOUR HOME REQUIRES YOU TO THROW OPEN THE CURTAINS AND LET THE SUNLIGHT IN, OR THEY WILL DIE. PLANTS MEAN VITAMIN D!

PLANTS NEED LOVE: THEY ARE THE PRE-PUPPY STEP. **2** IF YOU CAN'T KEEP A PLANT ALIVE, YOU'RE NOT READY FOR A DOG!

KEEPING A PLANT ALIVE GIVES YOU PRIDE IN YOUR NEWFOUND ABILITY TO SHARE YOUR LIVING SPACE WITH LIVING THINGS.

9

**3** PLANTS CLEAN THE AIR: THESE DAYS WE SPEND A LOT OF TIME INDOORS. IF YOU ARE FAMILIAR WITH THE PRINCIPLES OF FENG SHUI, YOU'LL KNOW THAT STALE AIR IS TERRIBLY BAD CHI! PLANTS DO THAT AMAZING THING OF SUCKING IN CARBON DIOXIDE AND PUMPING OUT SWEET, SWEET OXYGEN.

**4** PLANTS MAKE A ROOM! IF YOU CARE ABOUT MAKING A CHIC HOME, YOUR WORK IS NOT COMPLETE WITHOUT A FEW PLANT BABIES. THEY ADD MUCH-NEEDED COLOR AND TEXTURE TO A ROOM.

# STARTING *your* INDOOR GARDEN

# Equipment

RAISING HOUSEPLANTS ISN'T DIFFICULT BUT IT REQUIRES A FEW TOOLS. NOT ALL OF THEM ARE NECESSARY, BUT THEY CERTAINLY MAKE KEEPING PLANTS A LITTLE EASIER.

## SPRAY BOTTLE

HANDY FOR WATERING BONSAI AND SMALL PLANTS

## SCISSORS

FOR TRIMMING LEAVES AND TAKING CUTTINGS

## WATERING CAN

TO WATER YOUR PLANT BABIES

## GARDENING GLOVES

TO KEEP YOUR HANDS CLEAN AND SAFE FROM SPIKY PLANTS

## KITCHEN TONGS

HELPFUL WHEN TAKING
CACTI CUTTINGS

## YOUR HANDS

DUH!

## TEASPOON

ACTS LIKE A
SHOVEL FOR
MINI PLANTS

## HAND TOOLS

FOR FILLING POTS WITH
POTTING MIX

## CONTAINERS

TO HOUSE YOUR
JUNGLE

15

# POTTING MIX:

# WHAT IS THE

# difference?

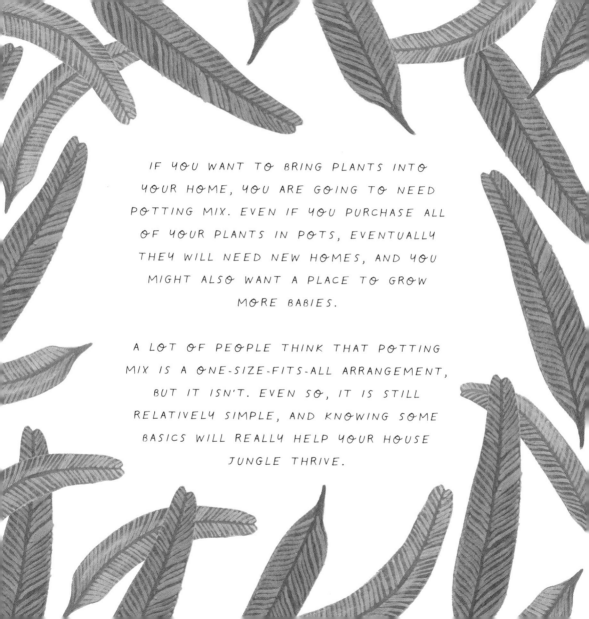

IF YOU WANT TO BRING PLANTS INTO YOUR HOME, YOU ARE GOING TO NEED POTTING MIX. EVEN IF YOU PURCHASE ALL OF YOUR PLANTS IN POTS, EVENTUALLY THEY WILL NEED NEW HOMES, AND YOU MIGHT ALSO WANT A PLACE TO GROW MORE BABIES.

A LOT OF PEOPLE THINK THAT POTTING MIX IS A ONE-SIZE-FITS-ALL ARRANGEMENT, BUT IT ISN'T. EVEN SO, IT IS STILL RELATIVELY SIMPLE, AND KNOWING SOME BASICS WILL REALLY HELP YOUR HOUSE JUNGLE THRIVE.

# ALL-PURPOSE POTTING MIX

MOST HOUSEPLANTS CAN EASILY
BE PLANTED AND REPOTTED USING
ALL-PURPOSE POTTING MIX.
HOWEVER, SOME PLANTS, SUCH
AS FERNS, HYACINTHS, AND TULIPS,
NEED MORE ACIDIC POTTING MIX
TO THRIVE. BE SURE TO READ
YOUR PLANT LABEL, PERUSE THE
OPTIONS AT THE GARDEN CENTER,
AND CHOOSE THE RIGHT MIX FOR
YOUR PLANTS.

# CACTI & SUCCULENT POTTING MIX

SUCCULENTS AND CACTI ARE POPULAR CHOICES FOR HOUSEPLANTS, BUT NOT EVERYBODY KNOWS THAT THEY NEED A PARTICULAR POTTING MIX THAT HAS MORE SAND AND STONES IN IT. IT ALLOWS WATER TO DRAIN BETTER. YOU CAN MIX YOUR OWN, BUT BUYING IT IS CERTAINLY EASIEST.

WHEN YOU START UP A LITTLE HOUSE JUNGLE OF YOUR OWN, YOU MIGHT WANT TO REPOT THE PLANTS YOU BRING HOME. MANY COMMERCIAL PLANTS ARE A BIT TOO COZY IN THEIR POTS AND WILL BE HAPPY TO HAVE A SLIGHTLY LARGER "APARTMENT." YOUR DÉCOR WILL BENEFIT FROM CONTAINERS THAT ARE PRETTIER THAN STANDARD PLASTIC POTS.

MOST PLANTS NEED A CONTAINER WITH DRAINAGE HOLES SO THEY DON'T BECOME WATERLOGGED. PLASTIC AND CERAMIC POTS WILL KEEP THE SOIL MOIST FOR LONGER, BUT SUCCULENTS AND CACTI OFTEN FARE BETTER IN TERRA-COTTA POTS, WHICH LET THE SOIL DRY OUT MORE QUICKLY. A NEW CONTAINER SHOULD BE AN INCH OR TWO LARGER ALL AROUND THAN THE LAST, TO GIVE ROOTS ROOM TO GROW.

YOUR PLANTS WILL ALSO NEED DISHES OR TRAYS TO PROTECT YOUR SURFACES FROM WATER. ANOTHER OPTION IS TO NESTLE THE PLASTIC POT WITHIN A PRETTIER CONTAINER. MAKE SURE TO EMPTY ANY EXCESS THAT COLLECTS HERE TO PREVENT PLANTS FROM SITTING IN WATER.

# CONTAINERS

# storing your EQUIPMENT

ACCUMULATING THE THINGS YOU NEED FOR
REARING YOUR OWN HOUSE JUNGLE ISN'T EXACTLY
CUMBERSOME, BUT YOU MIGHT FIND YOU NEED
SOMEWHERE TO STORE SOME OF THE DIRTIER
THINGS. IF YOU ARE LUCKY ENOUGH TO HAVE SOME
OUTDOOR SPACE, A MINIATURE PVC GREENHOUSE
IS IDEAL FOR STORING WATERING CANS, POTTING
MIX, AND SPARE POTS. IF NOT, STORING THINGS
IN A CUPBOARD OR CELLAR, WITH THE POTTING MIX
SEALED, WILL DO FINE.

# DECORATING WITH HOUSE PLANTS

# LONG, TRAILING
## PLANTS

PLANTS THAT GROW OVER THE EDGE OF THE
CONTAINER AND TUMBLE DOWNWARD (SUCH
AS STRING-OF-PEARLS PLANTS AND IVY) CAN BE
GREAT PIECES TO ADD COLOR TO UNEXPECTED
AREAS OF YOUR HOME. PLACE THEM ON A HIGH
SHELF FOR A BEAUTIFUL, STREAMING COLUMN OF
COLOR THAT'S A LITTLE MORE ADVENTUROUS
THAN A GENERIC POTTED PLANT.

# LARGE, ARCHITECTURAL PLANTS

FICUS, YUCCA, AND PALMS LOOK GREAT IN LARGE SIZES. THEIR NATURAL FORM OFFERS A PRETTY CONTRAST TO THE UNIFORMITY OF SHELVES AND FURNISHINGS, AND THEY ADD A BRIGHT SPLASH OF COLOR. EXPERIMENT WITH PLACING THE POTS IN COOL CONTAINERS SUCH AS BASKETS AND LINEN "BAGS."

# HANGING PLANTS

MACRAMÉ HAS COME BACK INTO FASHION, AND
WITH IT A GREAT WAY TO DECORATE WITH
HOUSEPLANTS. THERE ARE LOTS OF HANGING
PLANTERS OUT THERE TO TURN YOUR PLANTS INTO
WALL ART. (OR YOU COULD HAVE A GO AT MAKING
ONE YOURSELF!) THESE LOOK FANTASTIC WITH
SCULPTURAL SUCCULENTS AND TRAILING PLANTS.
HANDY WHEN YOU RUN OUT OF SURFACES TO
PUT PLANTS ON!

# decorating from the Garden

ANOTHER SIMPLE WAY TO BRING THE JOY OF
PLANTS INTO YOUR HOME IS THROUGH EXPLORING
WHAT'S OUTSIDE. WE DON'T HAVE TO SETTLE FOR
RAPIDLY WILTING FLOWERS; TAKE A LOOK AT THE
BRANCHES AND SPRIGS OF YOUR NEIGHBORHOOD AND
BEYOND! I FIND THAT LEAFY FOLIAGE (EUCALYPTUS,
PARTICULARLY) LASTS MUCH LONGER AND PROVIDES
THE "FRESH" FEELINGS HOUSEPLANTS GIVE, WITH
LESS RESPONSIBILITY.

# CARING FOR YOUR HOUSE PLANTS

# NORTH, SOUTH, EAST & WEST FACING WINDOWS

SOME PLANTS NEED MORE LIGHT THAN OTHERS, AND ONE THING THAT INFLUENCES WHERE YOU CAN KEEP DIFFERENT PLANTS IS THE DIRECTION YOUR HOME FACES. IT IS BEST TO FIGURE OUT WHICH WINDOWS GET THE MOST LIGHT.

THE SUN RISES IN THE EAST AND SETS IN THE WEST, SO LOOKING OUT OF YOUR WINDOWS AND CHECKING THE POSITION OF THE SUN SHOULD HELP YOU DETERMINE WHICH WAY YOUR WINDOWS FACE.

EAST- AND WEST-FACING WINDOWS WILL NATURALLY GET A PORTION OF SHADE THROUGHOUT THE DAY. FOR NORTHERN HEMISPHERE DWELLERS, SOUTH-FACING WINDOWS WILL GET THE STRONG SUNLIGHT, WHILE IN THE SOUTHERN HEMISPHERE, NORTH-FACING WINDOWS WILL.

# UNDER WATERING & OVER WATERING

## underwatered

CLOSE UP, THE SIGNS OF AN UNDERWATERED
PLANT ARE FAIRLY WELL KNOWN — STEMS
WILL DROOP, AND LEAVES WILL TURN BROWN
AND CRISPY AND DROP OFF. IF THE SOIL HAS
SEPARATED FROM THE EDGES OF THE POT,
IT'S TOO DRY!

## overwatered

OVERWATERING CAN LEAD TO ROOT ROT
AND A DEAD PLANT! SIGNS OF OVERWATERING
CAN INCLUDE YELLOW SPOTS, A MOLDY STEM,
AND DYING LEAVES. OVERWATERING IS MORE
OFTEN CAUSED BY TOO-FREQUENT WATERING
THAN TOO MUCH AT ONCE.

# Fertilizer

A PLANT THAT IS LOOKING A LITTLE YELLOW
AND DROPPING ITS LEAVES MAY NEED SOME
FERTILIZER ONCE IT HAS USED UP THE
NUTRIENTS IN THE SOIL.

YOU CAN FERTILIZE A PLANT UP TO ONCE
A MONTH WITH A HOUSEPLANT FERTLIZER,
BUT HOLD OFF IN WINTER MONTHS WHEN
THE PLANT IS DORMANT. FOLLOW THE
DIRECTIONS ON THE LABEL.

FERTILIZER

# CONGRATS!

NOW THAT YOU HAVE
THE BASIC KNOWLEDGE REQUIRED
TO NOT MURDER YOUR PLANTS,
IT'S TIME TO TAKE A LOOK AT
A FEW DIFFERENT TYPES TO
POPULATE YOUR NEW HOUSE
JUNGLE.

# TYPES OF HOUSE PLANTS

CACTI AND SUCCULENTS MAKE GREAT
HOUSEPLANTS. THEY ARE GROUPED
TOGETHER BECAUSE THEY GENERALLY
HAVE SIMILAR CARE REQUIREMENTS. MOST
CACTI AND SUCCULENTS ORIGINATE FROM
THE DESERT AND TYPICALLY REQUIRE
BRIGHT LIGHT AND LITTLE WATER. THEY
ARE ADAPTED TO STORE LOTS OF WATER
IN THEIR LEAVES AND "STEMS."

# CACTI &
# SUCCULENTS

SUCCULENTS THAT DON'T GET ENOUGH LIGHT MAY "STRETCH OUT" AND GET ODDLY TALL. THIS CAN BE REMEDIED BY CUTTING OFF THE TOP OF THE PLANT AND GROWING A NEW ONE. SEE PAGE 94 TO LEARN MORE.

# COMMON MISCONCEPTION

LOTS OF PEOPLE THINK THAT CACTI AND SUCCULENTS REQUIRE NO WATER. WHILE IT IS TRUE THAT THEY ARE ADAPTED TO EXIST ON LITTLE WATER FOR A LONG TIME, SUCCULENTS AND CACTI BENEFIT FROM A WATERING APPROXIMATELY ONCE A WEEK, LESS IN WINTER. SET THEM IN A BRIGHT WINDOW, AND DON'T ALLOW THEM TO SIT IN WATER.

BONSAI ARE SLIGHTLY MORE COMPLEX PLANTS BUT ARE
STILL DESERVING OF A SPOT IN YOUR HOUSE JUNGLE.
BONSAI ARE ESSENTIALLY MINI TREES, SO CARE IS
OFTEN SPECIFIC TO THE VARIETY. THEY CAN BE TRICKY
TO MANAGE, BUT IF YOU FOLLOW THE INSTRUCTIONS
CAREFULLY, YOU MAY HAVE YEARS OF SUCCESS. BONSAI
GENERALLY NEED WELL-DRAINING STONY POTTING
MIX. NEVER ALLOW A BONSAI TO EITHER DRY OUT
COMPLETELY OR TO SIT IN SATURATED SOIL.

DUE TO THEIR SMALL POTS, BONSAI REQUIRE MORE
FREQUENT FERTILIZATION. THE PROPER FOOD
CAN BE BOUGHT ONLINE AND COMES WITH
INSTRUCTIONS.

# BAM BOO

LIKE BONSAI, BAMBOO IS A SLIGHTLY TRICKIER
HOUSEPLANT THAT REQUIRES KNOWING THE
PARTICULAR SPECIES IN ORDER TO CARE FOR
IT APPROPRIATELY. WHEN PURCHASING, TAKE NOTE
OF THE VARIETY, OR ELSE USE IDENTIFICATION
GUIDES TO HELP. (THE INTERNET IS FULL OF
HELP WITH IDENTIFYING PLANTS.)

IN GENERAL, HOWEVER, BAMBOO SHOULD BE
PLANTED IN A POT WITH GOOD DRAINAGE, FAIRLY
CLOSE TO THE TOP OF THE SOIL, IN A WELL-
DRAINING POTTING MIX. THEY GENERALLY NEED
WATERING DAILY AND BENEFIT FROM A SPRITZ
WITH A SPRAY BOTTLE. BAMBOO SHOULD BE
FERTILIZED ONCE A YEAR WITH A HIGH-NITROGEN,
SLOW-RELEASE FERTILIZER.

air
plants

AIR PLANTS ARE FANTASTIC ADDITIONS TO YOUR HOUSE JUNGLE! THOUGH THEY REQUIRE MORE UNUSUAL CARE THAN A STANDARD POTTED PLANT, THEY ARE A FORGIVING SPECIES AND HAVE WONDERFUL DÉCOR POSSIBILITIES.

AIR PLANTS DO NOT REQUIRE SOIL, SO THEY CAN BE HUNG/ PLACED/BALANCED ALMOST ANYWHERE. THEY STILL NEED WATER, THOUGH; IT'S JUST THAT RATHER THAN WATERING A POT, YOU NEED TO SOAK THE WHOLE PLANT. AIR PLANTS ARE HAPPY IN LOWER LIGHT, WHICH MEANS THEY MAKE GREAT DÉCOR ADDITIONS.

UPON PURCHASING, YOUR AIR PLANT WILL PROBABLY NEED A GOOD SOAK. PLACE IT IN A BOWL OF WATER FOR 20 MINUTES OR SO, THEN SHAKE IT OFF THOROUGHLY AND PUT IT ON DISPLAY! REPEAT ONCE A WEEK. OVER TIME, AIR PLANTS WILL PRODUCE OFFSHOOT BABIES THAT RESEMBLE A SMALL VERSION OF THE MAIN PLANT. THESE CAN BE TWISTED OFF GENTLY TO MAKE A WHOLE NEW PLANT!

**TIP:** BROWN LEAF TIPS CAN SIGNAL UNDERWATERING, OR CHLORINE IN THE WATER. TRY LEAVING THE WATER TO SIT OVERNIGHT BEFORE SOAKING. A YELLOWY-GREEN LEAF THAT IS FALLING APART COULD WELL BE A SIGN OF OVERWATERING.

# RAINFOREST PLANTS

SOME POPULAR CHOICES FOR INDOOR RAINFOREST PLANTS ARE BROMELIADS, PHILODENDRON, FICUS, AND PEACE LILY.

RAINFOREST PLANTS LIKE ORCHIDS AND MONSTERA DELICIOSA ARE OFTEN CHARACTERIZED BY THICK, SPRAWLING ROOTS AND LARGE LEAVES THAT MAKE THE MOST OF THE LIGHT IN A SHADY FOREST.

TROPICAL HOUSEPLANTS DO BEST IN WARM AND HUMID ENVIRONMENTS. A SPRITZ OF WATER ALL OVER AND A QUICK DUSTING OF THE LEAVES WILL HELP THEM FLOURISH! RAINFOREST PLANTS NEED BRIGHT, INDIRECT SUNLIGHT AND REGULAR WATERING. ALLOW THE SOIL TO BECOME JUST DRY TO THE TOUCH FIRST.

# HERBS

## TIP:

BASIL IS A GREAT CHOICE FOR THE LESS
GREEN-THUMBED OF PLANT OWNERS
BECAUSE IT TELLS YOU WHEN IT NEEDS
A DRINK BY WILTING A LITTLE, THEN
PERKING RIGHT UP WHEN IT'S WATERED.

MOST PEOPLE WILL BE FAMILIAR WITH THE
HUMBLE HERB PLANT, OFTEN PURCHASED IN
CELLOPHANE AT THE SUPERMARKET. HERBS
ARE REWARDING TO KEEP BECAUSE THEY ADD
FLAVOR AND COLOR TO YOUR FOOD AS WELL
AS YOUR HOUSE!

IF YOU BUY HERBS FROM THE SUPERMARKET,
IT IS A GOOD IDEA TO PLANT THEM INTO
ANOTHER POT WITH MORE ROOM.

MOST HERBS NEED A WARM ROOM AND
WATERING ONCE THE TOP LAYER OF SOIL
IS DRY. HERBS NEED LOTS OF LIGHT AND
WILL BENEFIT FROM HAVING THEIR POTS
TURNED REGULARLY FOR EVEN SUN EXPOSURE.

# HOW TO CUT HERBS FOR COOKING

YOU JUST TAKE THE SCISSORS AND CUT THEM, RIGHT?

RIGHT, BUT IT'S BEST TO CUT STALKS FROM THE TOP (DON'T TAKE THE BIG LEAVES FROM THE BOTTOM! THOSE ARE THE BIGGEST LIGHT-CATCHERS) AND CUT THE STALK JUST ABOVE A PAIR OF LEAVES. THIS MEANS YOUR PLANT WILL FOCUS ITS ENERGY ON GROWING OUTWARD — WHICH MEANS BIGGER HERBS!

61

# plants _THAT_ tolerate Shade

# SNAKE PLANT

### SANSEVIERIA TRIFASCIATA

WATER ONLY WHEN SOIL FEELS DRY TO THE TOUCH.
POSITION OUT OF DIRECT SUN; PREFERS INDIRECT LIGHT.

# ARECA PALM

ARECA CATECHU

WATER ENOUGH TO KEEP THE SOIL SLIGHTLY MOIST IN
SPRING AND SUMMER; ALLOW SOIL TO DRY OUT BETWEEN
WATERINGS IN AUTUMN AND WINTER.

# SPIDER PLANT

## CHLOROPHYTUM COMOSUM

DOES WELL IN BRIGHT FLUORESCENT LIGHT OR IN INDIRECT SUNLIGHT. WATER ONCE SOIL BECOMES DRY TO THE TOUCH.

# PEACE LILY

## SPATHIPHYLLUM SPECIES

KEEP THE SOIL MOIST BUT NOT SATURATED,
AND KEEP IN A WARM ROOM.

# SWISS CHEESE PLANT

### MONSTERA DELICIOSA

ALLOW SOIL TO BECOME DRY TO THE TOUCH BETWEEN
WATERINGS. BENEFITS FROM AN OCCASIONAL SPRITZ OF
WATER TO THE LEAVES.

# plants THAT like Sunshine

# GOLDEN BARREL
## CACTUS

ECHINOCACTUS GRUSONII

WATER WHEN SOIL IS DRY IN SPRING AND SUMMER, BUT GIVE
ALMOST NO WATER OVER WINTER.

# MEXICAN HEN & CHICKS

*ECHEVERIA SPECIES*

WATER WHENEVER SOIL IS DRY IN SPRING AND SUMMER.
WATER ONLY IF IT LOOKS LIKE IT'S DYING OVER WINTER!

# ALOE VERA

ALOE VERA

WATER ONLY WHEN SOIL IS DRY IN SPRING AND SUMMER
AND EVEN LESS OVER WINTER.

# JADE PLANT

## CRASSULA OVATA

WATER WHEN THE SOIL SURFACE FEELS DRY, BUT NEVER LET THE SOIL DRY OUT COMPLETELY. BE MINDFUL OF OVERWATERING, TOO, THOUGH: IT WILL CAUSE ROOT ROT.

# YUCCA

YUCCA ELEPHANTIPES

NEEDS WARMTH! WATER AROUND EVERY 10 DAYS.
CAN SUFFER FROM OVERWATERING.

# HOUSE PLANTS THAT CAN TAKE ABUSE

# RUBBER TREE

*FICUS ELASTICA*

PREFERS INDIRECT SUNLIGHT. WARNS YOU WITH
YELLOWY-BROWN LEAVES IF YOU'RE OVERWATERING!

# CAST IRON PLANT

ASPIDISTRA ELATIOR

IT IS HAPPY IN LOW LIGHT AND WILL SURVIVE IF YOU
FORGET TO WATER IT FOR A BIT.

# SCARLET STAR

GUZMANIA LINGULATA

A MEMBER OF THE BROMELIAD FAMILY, IT CAN SURVIVE IN
MEDIUM LIGHT AND PUT UP WITH FORGETFUL WATERERS.

# ENGLISH IVY

HEDERA HELIX

IN THE WILD IT'S CONSIDERED A WEED BECAUSE IT REFUSES
TO DIE! COPES WITH COLD SPOTS AND OVERWATERING.

# CHINESE EVERGREEN

AGLAONEMA COMMUTATUM

TOLERATES POOR LIGHT, DRY AIR, AND DROUGHT!

# DRAGON TREE

DRACAENA MARGINATA

THIS COMMON PLANT WILL SOLDIER ON THROUGH SHADY
ROOMS AND CARELESS WATERING.

# ZEBRA CACTUS

HAWORTHIA ATTENUATA

A SMALL SUCCULENT THAT COPES WITH OVERZEALOUS
WATERERS AND POOR LIGHT. TURNS MAROON WHEN IT'S
THIRSTY!

# INCH PLANT

TRADESCANTIA ZEBRINA

WILL STILL GROW FURIOUSLY, EVEN WHEN OVER- OR UNDERWATERED.

# ZZ PLANT

ZAMIOCULCAS ZAMIIFOLIA

CAN SURVIVE SERIOUS NEGLECT WITHOUT BATTING
AN EYELID.

# PRAYER PLANT

MARANTA LEUCONEURA

TOLERATES LOW LIGHT.

# WAX PLANT

### HOYA CARNOSA

WILL GROW IN LOW LIGHT, BUT WON'T BLOOM. TOLERATES
FORGETFUL WATERERS.

# HEART LEAF
# PHILODENDRON

PHILODENDRON SCANDENS

SURVIVES HAPPILY IN A TOO-SMALL POT AND IS EASY TO
PROPAGATE FROM CUTTINGS.

# DEVIL'S IVY

### EPIPREMNUM AUREUM

LOSES ITS YELLOW VARIEGATION IF IT'S NOT GETTING
ENOUGH LIGHT.

# BIRD'S NEST FERN

*ASPLENIUM NIDUS*

CAN SURVIVE IN LOW LIGHT, BUT LEAVES WON'T
BE AS CRINKLY.

# where TO BUY Plants

NOW THAT YOU KNOW HOW TO TAKE CARE OF YOUR PLANTS, WE
SHOULD PROBABLY COVER WHERE TO GET SOME!

THE OBVIOUS CHOICE IS A LOCAL GARDEN CENTER, WHICH WILL
LIKELY HAVE THE BEST SELECTION. THERE ARE ALSO NURSERIES
THAT SPECIALIZE IN CERTAIN VARIETIES OF PLANT, SUCH AS CACTI,
THAT HAVE MANY CHOICES.

ADDITIONALLY, IT IS COMMON TO FIND
A DECENT SELECTION IN SUPERMARKETS,
HOME-SUPPLY STORES, LOCAL MARKETS,
AND CERTAIN SWEDISH FLAT-PACK
FURNITURE STORES! FLORISTS
OFTEN HAVE A NICE RANGE
OF SUCCULENTS AND OTHER
GREEN PLANTS, TOO.

FINALLY, A GREAT SELECTION OF
PLANTS CAN BE FOUND ONLINE,
WHETHER ON EBAY, AMAZON, OR A
DEDICATED ONLINE SUPPLIER. THIS
METHOD IS GREAT FOR SCORING
UNUSUAL PLANTS, BUT THE DOWNSIDE
IS NOT BEING ABLE TO LOOK THEM
OVER BEFORE PURCHASING.

# HOW TO Make MORE PLANTS

## (FOR FREE!)

# HOW TO PROPAGATE SUCCULENTS

SUCCULENTS ARE AMAZING BECAUSE THEY GROW THEIR OWN BABIES. YOU CAN GROW AN ENTIRELY NEW PLANT FROM A SINGLE LEAF! THIS IS CALLED PROPAGATING. HERE'S HOW.

SIMPLY TWIST OFF A LEAF GENTLY FROM A "PARENT PLANT." PROPAGATING IS A GREAT WAY TO RESCUE PARENT PLANTS THAT HAVE STRETCHED — SIMPLY START AGAIN WITH THEIR LEAVES.

LEAVE THE LEAF SOMEWHERE DRY FOR ABOUT A WEEK. THE "WOUND" WHERE YOU REMOVED THE LEAF NEEDS A CHANCE TO FORM A CALLUS.

AFTER A WEEK OR SO, PLACE THE LEAF ON A BED OF POTTING MIX. SPRITZ THE POTTING MIX EVERY FEW DAYS.

EVENTUALLY THE LEAF WILL SPROUT ROOTS.

 THEN THE LEAF WILL SPROUT MORE LEAVES!

KEEP SPRITZING WITH WATER UNTIL THE OLD
LEAF HAS WITHERED AND CAN BE GENTLY
TWISTED OFF.

PUT YOUR NEW TINY PLANT INTO SOME
SUCCULENT/CACTI POTTING MIX AND WATER
LIKE YOU WOULD ANY OTHER SUCCULENT.

 YOUR TINY PLANT WILL CONTINUE TO GROW
AND CAN BE PROPAGATED AGAIN!

CUT OFF HERE!

# TIP:

THIS PROCESS CAN ALSO BE USED
TO SAVE THE VERY TOP OF A
STRETCHED "ROSETTE" SUCCULENT
(SUCH AS ECHEVERIA).

SIMPLY CUT OFF THE "ROSE" AT
THE TOP OF THE STRETCHED STEM
AND FOLLOW THE SAME STEPS.

ADDITIONALLY, IF YOU CONTINUE TO
CARE FOR THE STEM YOU CUT IT
FROM, IT WILL BLOOM NEW BABIES
CLOSER TO THE SOIL.

# HOW TO TAKE CUTTINGS

MANY OTHER PLANTS CAN BE CUT AND GROWN INTO NEW PLANTS. SOME PLANTS ROOT BETTER THAN OTHERS, SO IT IS WISE TO DO SOME RESEARCH ON YOUR PLANT, OR SIMPLY BE PREPARED FOR SOME TRIAL AND ERROR.

MANY PLANTS WILL GROW ROOTS FROM THE NODES ON
THE STEMS. VINING, TRAILING PLANTS ARE THE EASIEST
TO GROW FROM CUTTINGS. CUTTINGS FROM PLANTS WITH
WOODY STEMS NEED A LITTLE EXTRA WORK.

TO PROPAGATE A TRAILING PLANT, CUT A PIECE SEVERAL INCHES FROM THE ENDS OF THE VINES. STRIP OFF THE LEAVES AT THE BOTTOM OF THE CUTTING, LEAVING A FEW IN PLACE. PUT THE CUTTINGS IN A GLASS OF WATER AND SET IT IN A WARM SPOT WITH INDIRECT LIGHT. WHEN IT SPROUTS A ROOT OR TWO, YOU CAN POT THE CUTTINGS INTO A SMALL POT TO MAKE A NEW PLANT!

WITH OTHER KINDS OF PLANTS, CUT A FEW STEMS SEVERAL INCHES LONG. CUT JUST ABOVE A SET OF LEAVES WHERE THE STEM IS SOFTER AND NOT WOODY. REMOVE A FEW LEAVES AND DIP THE CUT ENDS IN ROOTING POWDER (THIS CAN BE FOUND ONLINE OR AT A GARDEN CENTER), THEN PLANT THEM IN A SMALL POT OF POTTING MIX. WATER AND SET IN A WARM SPOT WITH INDIRECT LIGHT. A CLEAR PLASTIC BAG CAN HELP KEEP THE HUMIDITY IN, BUT DON'T LET THE PLANT GET TOO SOGGY. ONCE THE CUTTINGS HAVE ROOTED, TAKE OFF THE BAG.